ALICE AND THE NORTH

Anne Caldwell is a freelance writer and education specialist, based in West Yorkshire. She has worked for the British Council as their Literature Programme Manager, and currently works for the Open University as an Associate Lecturer in Creative Writing, whilst also undertaking a PhD in prose poetry at The University of Bolton.

Her poetry has appeared in a range of anthologies in the UK and internationally, in magazines including *Writing Women*, *The North*, *Poetry Wales* and *Stride*, and in three collections including *Painting the Spiral Staircase* (Cinnamon Press, 2016). In 2019, she was co-editor of *The Valley Press Anthology of Prose Poetry*, alongside Oz Hardwick.

Alice and the North

ANNE CALDWELL

Valley Press

First published in 2020 by Valley Press
Woodend, The Crescent, Scarborough, YO11 2PW
www.valleypressuk.com

ISBN 978-1-912436-52-1
Cat. no. VP0173

Cover design by Fitzpatrick Designs.
Text design by Peter Barnfather.
Edited by Martha Sprackland.

Printed and bound in Great Britain by
Imprint Digital, Upton Pyne, Exeter.

Contents

Dedicated to Bertha Alice Caldwell

I would like to thank Simon Holloway, David Rudd, Ben Wilkinson, Amanda Dalton, Liz Almond, Andy Melrose, Char March, Andrew Forster, Vicki Feaver, Jane Feaver, Lindsey Holland, Carola Luther, Martha Sprackland and members of the IPSI project based at the University of Canberra for all their help and inspiration.

I would also like to thank fellow students from the 'clusters and entanglements' group for their support and generosity.

Alice and The Borders

The North is a weaving bed, shifting sand, a river cleaving Picts from Scots where the law is thin. Alice is trying to draw the border. Raided by Reivers, the rules here are whippets. The fort at Housesteads is collapsing. And where is her spine? Both sides? Where are her kith and kin? Can she see between the sheep and goats, find a bloodline on a map or border on her skin? England rattles like a portcullis and Scotland sharpens its sabres. She's looking for edges. Alice sketches the smell of heather burning, the echo of clogs, coal, and the black-faced ewes snaking through the gaps in Hadrian's wall.

Ferns and Voles

Alice doesn't have a looking-glass but there's a full-length mirror in her mother's room and a cat that refuses to smile. She's five and the world is full of wonder. She makes rose petal tea for her dolls, rabbit and stuffed tiger. Alice has a den in the bottom of her wardrobe that smells of plimsolls. She visits a treehouse at Sarah's in a crack willow where the branches fork and the sky falls in. Henny Penny run, run!

When it snows, Alice burrows in drifts like a vole and the world is crystalline and mauve. Ice ferns her bedroom window and she doesn't speak for days. She turns six and a baby sister appears. Alice makes a new den in the garage from two deckchairs, a broom and a grey felt blanket. She steals a packet of her sister's Farley's rusks and eats them out there on the concrete floor.

A chest freezer full of lamb carcasses and frozen veg hums in the corner. Somewhere in the house, her father is curled up like a caterpillar in an armchair, listening to Bach, his head wreathed in smoke.

Steel

There once were three sisters who lived on treacle: Elsie, Lacie and Tillie. This is the start of the Dormouse's story. Alice's siblings can't stand the stuff. All that sweetness.

She imagines her family as knives lying together in a cupboard drawer. They're a hard-edged bunch. Good at cutting up love into bite-sized chunks; slicing skin or soft fruit.

The knife with the serrated edge reminds her of her mother. Why? Something to do with gutting and scoring, loaves and fishes. The ability to produce a meal out of nothing. Her mother's small miracles, night after night served up on china plates printed with chintz. Alice will sharpen the knives tomorrow after work. Sheffield steel is gleaming in a dark drawer lined with felt.

Rust and Nettles

Down, down, down.
Would the fall never come to an end?
– Lewis Carroll, *Alice's Adventures in Wonderland*

Alice and her sisters are fat from eating mulberries, blackberries, sloes and grassy, bitter damsons. Fingertips and lips stain purple. Their Tupperwares leak trails of juice. Boundary Lane is billowing with cow parsley. The girls feel like they're carrying a dismembered body home. Alice is reading *Little Women* and *The Hobbit*. The season is on the cusp. At night, they sleep closer together: four sisters blowsy with heat and sunburnt shoulders. They're skinny as wild cats, calloused from wandering barefoot. Soon Alice will slip on borrowed stilettos, smear her cheeks with rouge and the map of Wonderland will be gone forever. Her mother sterilises Kilner jars in the oven, purses her lips. She fills a larder with the summer's glut, slow-cooks meringue, brittle with love. *It can happen in an instant*, she says, darkly. Alice has some idea of what this means.

Congleton

The cul-de-sac is quiet. Gangs of distant roller-skaters trundle up and down the empty roads beyond. Alice grows in a bowl of wild-faced children. A rocket-shaped figure lurks in the ice-cream van with his deadnettle promises of Pyrex riches. He tells Alice to sit still on his lolly.

And down the lane lives Mr Riches the PE teacher who downs whisky, then lets his practised root hang loose and wet in his pants. Skin tight. Living purple. His girls run up and down the hockey pitch, bruising each other's ankles mauve.

In the distance, on the M6, goods lorries long to nuzzle, limp home as the motorway bridge hangs its head, pollen yellow. Alice decides she's a horse in a field. The grass is boggy with silver birch.

Moscow

Alice's father chokes on his first taste of Russian vodka. Minders escort him across Red Square, sweeping through the snow-bound city. An army of wrinkled women brushes up bottles and drunks.

Alice is too young to understand the early warning siren strapped to her school roof, or the words *deterrent, proliferation*. She kneels, as instructed, under her desk. When *Apollo 13* fails to land, her father comes home for once, throws his arms around his daughters. They watch the *Odyssey* splash down on a black and white TV. Astronauts emerge like Homer's heroes from the dark side of the moon.

In seventy-four, her father gives Alice a Babushka doll, then collapses on the sofa. The USSR tightens its grip like a nutcracker and people shrivel up behind curtains in Chechnya, Latvia and Ukraine. Alice lines up the wooden dolls, matched forearms and hands, screwed midriffs together, curves splitting in the over-heated house. Her father coughs blood into a cup. Mother stockpiles tins; warms Heinz tomato soup.

Crab Apples

Thousands of ladybirds are scrambling all over the privet, flitting from the honeysuckle to the crab apple tree, landing on her skin. Concrete slabs beneath the washing line, hot as waffles. Alice squashes the ladybirds and red spider mites without mercy, her boredom treacle thick. She thinks of the Dormouse in the teapot and those three sticky sisters at the bottom of the well.

She listens to the rhythmic bounce of a tennis ball against a wall. Long evenings of skating up and down the same damn street. Alice is standing next to a telephone box that smells of rotten fruit. She's trying to ring some boy without being overheard. Since her father's death, her family house is eiderdowned with grief.

Sheep's Clothing

A felled elm spreads out like a body on the ground with all its bare roots showing. Her father's music is scattered to the four winds. More storms roll in. She hears the words *Dutch elm disease* on the radio for the first time and senses the trees disappearing like friends from the hedgerows.

Alice thinks of a huntsman out in the woods beyond Congleton Edge. A dark well somewhere in the Peak District. Would she drown in her own tears? Pools are swimming with ducks, dodos, a lory and eaglet.

She dreams of a wolf in sheep's clothing. She doesn't know what that means. But she understands a gingerbread house. She knows you have to stick a chicken bone instead of a finger towards the grinning witch. She knows that much.

Will silence break into song? Things will never be the same again as she scatters bits of bread along the path and listens for a chaffinch or a blackbird or a coal-tit. She practices in her head an arpeggio of windblown nests and broken eggs.

Storm Brewing

The idea of a room becomes a moor; intimacy is as wide as a meadow. Alice doesn't know this place, or what she even understands by place. The pathway she finds leads back to the room. The room opens out and she finds herself next to a river. She cups water in her hands, bending to taste it, as the horizon is gashed by lightning. Straws of marram grass. Then the sky closes in like a room. Storm in a teacup perhaps? The ceiling is a wayward scribble.

Slow Train North

Alice leaves King's Cross and loses her mobile signal. She sits in the quiet coach as it rumbles through the hinterlands of the capital. Flats and terraced rows give way to avenues, semis with clipped privet. Here's the Lincolnshire flatlands – big skies, reed beds, wild ducks. Alice listens to the person opposite breathing, to the rhythm of the diesel engine and the whirr of an old heater in the carriage. Her coat's heavy with it. There's her reflection, bunched up like the March Hare caught by headlights somewhere in The Wolds. There's the warmth of her face against glass. The Wash sprays salt through an open window, and that pull north is stronger than ever. The Pole's magnetic embrace.

Maybe she'll cradle a block of ice and rip the skin off her fingertips. But right now, she's reading Louis MacNeice and this is the 'Slow Movement': the pause between opening and closing, the *allegro* and *appassionato*. This is where she sits. Between the city and the icebergs, the heat and that stretch of winter. No sun for three months. She's just passing, finding joy in the view from the window: wetlands alive with trout, fireflies dancing, rookeries chattering and their offspring plump with love.

Southern Border, Staffordshire

She thinks of all the people she's seen reflected
in shop windows. Her mother, stone-hearted
and frazzled with chores, the shadow of her
dead father and his black umbrella, her three
sisters arguing as usual, with bright red gloves
and sour faces. There's the reflection of Mr
Greenwood with a false leg, who ran the bacon
and cheese shop. She remembers oatcakes and
pikelets. Working for him on a Saturday,
slicing Parma ham for the Italian restaurant,
then weighing out slivers of torta di Dolcelatte.

Thirty years later, her knuckles are still scarred.
Alice could have been a small-town butcher's
wife. Instead, she muffles the past and sleeps
under woollen blankets from a charity shop.
She has bolted the front door but those
reflections slide, belly-up, into night hours.
There's the Mock Turtle, a Duchess and a
baby. Her feet begin to swell and she clutches
a feather pillow to her breasts.

St Anne's on Sea, Western Border

Miss Batho's fragile as a damselfly in her blue-tinted spectacles. Aunt Bertha is a walnut, dressed in jet and lace. When she walks, clouds of dry skin catch the afternoon light. Alice and her sisters are allowed to perch on a velvet pouffe. This is the land of genteel poverty, seaside bungalows staring towards the west.

A French clock charts their every move from under its glass dome. Like the Queen of Hearts, Aunt Bertha removes a key on a chain from deep within her bodice. She swings open a cabinet crammed with porcelain and cranberry glass. Blue and white Chinese figures dance across bridges before the girls' eyes. Miss Batho leans forwards. Alice is scared she'll topple, shatter like bone china.

Spurn Point, Eastern Border

Alice holds onto names of the North as if they are little loaves and fishes. They comfort her as she stirs her tea. Names of family members, rose varieties, edible fungi. Names from the classroom come flooding back to her: Elizabeth Evans, Hazel Soper, Katherine Turner, Christopher Tew. Nouns fly over the mudflats – warblers, shrikes, wrynecks, egrets, redwings fieldfares, blackbirds, song thrush. An occasional merlin.

If the planet continues to warm, this place will be a snake's tongue, swallowing itself once more. As she walks towards the lighthouse, she thinks of what it might be like to be imprisoned, scratching a five-bar-gate of days into a wall or writing poems with a matchstick into soap; memorised and then scrubbed out like dirty linen.

A shingle of words piles up and she draws them with a stick in the wet sand, just above the high tideline. *Slack Top, Congleton, Kinder Scout, Scar Fell, Pecket Well, Erringdon, Ambleside, Malham, Kettlewell, Wetwang, Buxton.* Her life laid out before her like grey skin cells – flattened, then rubbed out by the incoming tide.

Bedrock

Alice is walking high on the moors, away from the flood warnings. She's living with curlews and skylarks in a land sculpted by wind. Its people are millstone grit, shale and limestone. Stratified and glacial.

There's a fire roaring in her old house and a mullion-silence. The air is quiet and thick as the first snowfall on the tops. The place smells of cinnamon and cloves. She sleeps in, wanders through the empty rooms in a red dressing gown and slippers. She longs for warmth and company: a tea party or a game of croquet with pink flamingos.

Jerusalem Farm is up for sale and the New Delight is short of drinkers. This is the land of miracles but this year they're as thin on the ground as lapwings' eggs.

Election Night

Deep within the folds of the Pennines, Alice watches the news on TV. America is a light-bulb, unshaded; it's a room laid bare in all its ugliness, full of plastic furniture and straight-backed chairs. A room you walk into when you want to lock the door and keep the world at bay. There are stars and stripes across the walls and nowhere comfortable to rest.

This room has bars on the windows. If you lift a corner of the carpet, you'll see prejudice cockroaching across the floors.

Off with their heads! he shouts. After a long night of no sleep is this where people have chosen to gather and celebrate?

Bird on a Wire

'It doesn't matter which way you go,' said the Cat.
'– so long as I get SOMEWHERE,' Alice added as an explanation.
'Oh, you're sure to do that,' said the Cat, 'if you only walk long enough.'
– Lewis Carroll, *Alice's Adventures in Wonderland*

And maybe the way forward is this unexpected winter sun and the cat asleep on her kitchen table; maybe the way forward is a kettle humming and peppermint tea, pale as longing in a cup; maybe forward is all those Facebook good wishes and kisses. And maybe it's an iPad with a broken screen that she can't afford to fix, but which still works; maybe the way forward is listening to Ali Smith on the radio as Leonard Cohen dies and her student has discovered his music without her help.

Maybe the way forward is the familiar path to Stoodley Pike, up beyond the lambing fields and the last working farm. And may be and may be and for and for and ward off all the ghosts please. #longing, as long as you have music and stories.

Blue Manchester

The moon didn't rise tonight. The city's reach pulled her; the sun burned without diminishing. There was poetry on the radio as blue Monday drifted into Tuesday, Wednesday. When she caught the clock with outstretched hands, she took her sharpened pencil as a companion. Good wood. *I have now revised a poem to make it more specific*, she said to herself. She recycled, signed petitions, pictured her lover pressed against her in a busy Caffè Nero. Remembered his sweat and his orange silk skirt.

Harleys and Gasometers

Alice was a puma padding up Corporation St, her pelt gleaming, soaked by days of rain. Salford's gutters were full to the brim. She dragged her choke-chain through the car parks and cobbled back-to-backs, shied from light spilling out of Bargain Booze, nosed the chip wrappers and polystyrene trays. All the while the drizzle came down. Her eyes reflected sodium glare, taxi hubcaps, winking tower blocks and a Lidl sign. No one noticed her slide on her belly under galvanised gates to sniff the man's Harley-Davidson, with its chrome curves, fumes and engine ticking from a wet commute. The stitched seat was sleek and beautiful.

Trespass

Her eyes narrowed as he left his door ajar. He'd stepped out in the yard for a smoke, leathers rain-soaked. Alice slipped inside, warmed by carpet-pile, by the quiet of the house with its fine sightlines. Later, he straightened a print, sensed the shadow of something darker than himself.

The house smelt of freshly ground coffee, gallery paint. The kitchen hummed as he slept upstairs. She toppled a carton from the kitchen worktop, lapping with her rough tongue as milk dribbled and pooled on the tiled floor. The photographer shivered in his sleep, dreaming of a route across the Dakota plains. She brushed past the cacti on the windowsill, her flank bristling with filaments.

She cleared his stairs with a jump, smelt the warmth of his motorway-skin. He woke to find her draped across his shoulders; his collarbone scratched. As she licked the salt from his clavicle, he lay quite still. Listened to her tuned-up engine purr.

Northern Quarter

A glass of white wine and the thought of
the basement bar sends Alice out into the
streets, where the windscreens are iced and
pavements slippery with expectation. This is
the kind of night that Hopper painted: saloons,
coffee pit-stops, single men and women
drinking with their shoulders curved over a
bourbon. Cadillacs and Chryslers gliding like
stingrays on his boulevards. Or a night Djuna
Barnes knew well; full of one-night stands
and strip joints and neon signs.

But this is Manchester, not Paris or New York.
In Alabama's All-American Eatery, bagels are
boiling in vats, waiting for the early morning
rush of clubbers who have danced through
the small hours of ecstasy and coke. That
craving for something soft and sweet.

Alice slinks like a stray towards her fridge, to
gorge on triangles of cold pizza, plates of
cheese, dry crackers, toast and peanut butter as
the clock stares down and her lover slumbers
in the warmth of an upstairs quilt.

The Resilience of Dandelions

After the chill of the winter months, Alice waits for you at the corner of Great Bridgewater St with her face open to the sun. She thought she'd lost you: no phone signal, no A-Z, no charge. Alice had folded her arms against the desire paths of friendship or the route maps of lovers. But today, the city simmers with intimacy: students chat over espressos and a cherry tree is coming into bud. She listens to the low rumble of trains beneath her, the screeching of trams cutting their way across Piccadilly Gardens. Soon you'll stroll together through Chinatown, across St Peter's Square to the Central Library with its domed acoustics and marbled pillars. You'll talk of the resilience of dandelions pushing their yellow way through cracks in pavements.

The Last Wolf

*A carved stone by the side of the A9 near Brora claims
to mark the site where the last wolf in Sutherland
was killed by a man called Polson in 1700.*

And Alice won't write about snow, icicles on
the inside of her windows, relief after all that
hot, destructive rain. And she won't write about
letting a lover go – that fucking American
with his Harley and his Leica. His Alaskan
attitude to love. She won't write about the
Istanbul bombings near the Blue Mosque,
nor the Paris explosions.

She'll write about George Mackay Brown: his
awkward brilliance, fear of the female body
spilling over the cadences of Orkney. She is
brimful of his Catholic taste and whisky. The
Stromness wind is howling. As she reads, she's
beachcombing with George whilst the sickle
moon lies on its back.

The Far North

NOT here! the white North has thy bones; and thou,
Heroic sailor-soul,
Art passing on thine happier voyage now
Toward no earthly pole.
– Alfred, Lord Tennyson, 'Sir John Franklin',
Westminster Abbey Memorial

You wouldn't know the North if it came up and bit you on the butt, said her American friend one night. *Well, it depends how you define it,* Alice replied, rather too sharply. Much later, as he snored in the spare room, she tried to remember a student trip to the Far North. It was a map hidden somewhere in her limbic system. She'd travelled on the mail ship from Bergen to Bodo, up the crinkled coast of Norway. She could recall the boredom of days at sea, sailing in and out of countless fjords. Now the glaciers were retreating at an alarming rate. Tundra was no longer permafrost. Most of her memory was gone, like a set of sea charts, slightly foxed, stored in an attic.

The Piano

Troldhaugen. Birch trees with white trunks. Alice remembered a day trip to Grieg's house. There was his grand piano with its yellowing ivory keys. A small wooden shack where he composed music. Pale trunks, peeling bark. She thought of his Piano Concerto in A minor: a soundtrack to this endless summer half-light, the way the dark never quite materialised. Pale trunks and peeling bark. Later, she tuned in to the sorrowful beat of the ship's engine at night. She remembered the way the landscape took over and emptied of people the further north she went. Silence. Those mountains were arctic dreams, rising out of the black water. She remembered the scene where Jane Eyre curled up in the windowseat.

She pictured Mary Shelley's monster out on the ice. Conifers, brittle with acid rain, stretched as far as the eye could see and clapperboard villages clung to the coast like whelks.

Midnight Sun

There had been a beautiful Swedish man on the mail ship and the possibility of sex. He wore a long trenchcoat with a paperback copy of *Crime and Punishment* stuffed in the pocket. He was solemn, diffident, with such spots as young men have before they shave regularly. Alice was reading *The Bell Jar*. She thought of them making love under glass, their skin mottled with cold, mouthing words to each other like goldfish. *Come quickly. Fuck me, quick as a fox, my darling.*

Once Alice entered the Far North, the coast became rocky and lunar. The young man had disembarked and stared at her from the shore. But she was beyond the tree line. Rock and water and lichen. A metal globe on the cliffs marked the latitude of the Arctic Circle. Over the past fifty years, the annual mean temperature in Svalbard had increased by 3.2°C. The word to describe this light was 'gloaming'. Had she discovered this definition when reading Plath? Maybe. The word suited the nature of the journey.

Nidderdale

Back home, Alice made a nest of coats in the caravan she borrowed from a friend. She was off-grid. It rained all night, Nidderdale rain, heavy and persistent, drumming on the metal roof of her box-shaped room, with the sound of the river like a bass note in the music of water. Her father would have remarked, *it's raining stair rods, lass, or raining cats and dogs.* She thought of Escher's stairways leading nowhere, the Louise Bourgeois print of a woman cradling an angry baby at the bottom of a flight of steps.

At night she dreamt of stray terriers falling from the sky. Would she be *furred in*, rather than snowed in? Limp, sodden bodies piled up against the cinder blocks of the caravan? Waking to sunshine was a relief. She parted the yellow beaded curtain and looked up to the grit-stone moors, birch trees shimmering like unspoken words.

Felling

One evening, Set-Square Sid died quietly like a clinker-built boat leaving the shoreline. His nephew cut down five oak trees that shaded the terrace where Alice lived. She watched the branches being felled and shielded her ears as a chainsaw whined. Light flooded in, but no birdsong.

She played Grieg on her iPod. There were no acorns to collect in September and Crimsworth Dene's wind screamed up against the back-to-back cottages. Alice had *cherished* those oaks, with their stunted trunks and ability to cling to life when circumstances were thin. She drew them from memory but could not catch the way their sunlight had dappled her mullioned windows or the scent of them. That resin, earthy smell that signalled spring.

Antipodes

Alice emails her sister in Australia. She tells her, here, in the northern hemisphere, there's no ounce of warmth in the air. A bowl of white crocus comes into bloom in her front yard.

She texts the local farmer. There's a ewe stuck on its back in the lambing field. *Prolapsed womb*, he mutters. Alice winces. She watches as he grabs the sheep by the fleece, checks her hooves for rot and shoves her organs back into her body with a fist.

She tells her sister there's no room big enough in her worker's cottage to hold a man. She's tried and found herself crushed, like the woman in *The Yellow Wallpaper*. Her rooms are better at holding old maps, fishbones, dead conversations, sheep's skulls and the soft night-padding of stray cats. *There are things in the walls that nobody knows about but me, nor ever will.* She asks her sister to write of the progress of wasps and hornets; their black and yellow thoraxes; Antipodean heat vibrating in their wings.

Hebden Bridge Floods

Alice is fishing a flooded house out and finds
Jen's evening, a 4B pencil, a river's slip-crack of
pebbles, and then, whatever else – the washed-
out phrase. She finds the marshalled hours of
the loved late at night and those who finally
are leaving something. Alice finds Carrie, her
forehead pressed against cloth. She's been
scrubbing out a cellar on her hands and knees.
She finds a church hall, a cinema, a Little
Theatre thick with mud.

Sludge has settled in the tubas, cornets, horns
of the brass band, clogging bells, valve slides
and waterkeys. Alice sluices the feather pattern
of grasses on cellar walls. The imprint of
filthy water. The river breathes into her. It
breathes out a sediment-smell and still the
rain is coming down. This will happen again
as the earth heats. This much she knows.
Her empathy is with these flooded northern
people and places.

Nox

Many the peoples many the oceans I crossed –
I arrive at these poor, brother, burials
so I could give you the last gift owed to death
and talk (why?) with mute ash.
— Catullus, poem 101 (trans. Anne Carson)

And the next day language is a difficult ascent and defeats her for a while. She's in the swimming pool, early in the morning before the sun's up. Alice feels water rippling against her skin. Retired breast-strokers make their majestic passageway through the shallows. The front-crawlers occupy the fast lane: commuters who turn their heads sideways to take in air. Nobody's speaking and this is even more refreshing. Here, at least, water is chlorinated and contained.

Outside, there are winter hedgerows, rowan berries and abandoned fields. In her locker lies a crumpled letter from a lost lover, like a bruise hidden in the body.

Carson made *Nox* from crumpled paper and photographs of her dead brother. It's concertinaed somewhere on the bookshelves in Alice's house, alongside Les Murray, Selima Hill and miscellaneous books that don't quite fit on the upper shelves.

North West Passage

*When we travel, these spaces we fall into are
like oil droplets suspended in water.*
— Anne Carson, *Short Talks*

Alice folds her laptop and switches her iPhone to airplane mode. She is taking a night flight from London to Minneapolis, a flight that swallows hours. She's crossing time zones and Greenland tundra. As she sleeps, she thinks of Franklin and his ship, the *HMS Terror*. It's been found in pristine condition at the bottom of an Arctic bay. She pictures divers swimming through the mess hall, working their deep-sea way through cabins, opening a food storage room with six plates and one tin can on the barnacled shelves.

The ship's bell lies on its side in astonishment. There are wine bottles, tables, a desk with open drawers. One hundred and twenty-nine drowned men. Ancient mariners failing to tell their story, failing to find an elusive, lucrative route through the ice.

Winter

This house has been far out to sea all night,
— Ted Hughes, 'Wind'

Alice became Medusa – she was a line of
Heptonstall venom, she was the Craggs
spitting, hitting her house through all the
fire and felt and flags. Wind hissed Alice
through the mullions, wind solid as stone
walls. The roof hurried inside, the Velux
window turned to salt or was bent into a
Lowry figure. Hold on. She'd no coal. No
outhouse nor barbecue with that promise of
a summer-filled bowl. Magpies chattered across
the gimmer in their ash-buzzard dive.

Ted, she thought, you'd scoff at drones,
bombs and the Lycra men cycling. You'd
recognise this road or the in-comers, but
would you take up residence in the sheds
where Keighley was once measured by the
mills rolling, a day of fustian?

Lost Sheep

Saddleworth Moor was on fire that night. Arson. Alice drove home up from Littleborough, across Blackstone Edge, following the hill's spine. A line of flames licked the tarmac till it bubbled and melted. Smoke billowed across the hills, skirting the reservoir, obscuring pylons. Thick, black, acrid in the throat. Police and fire sirens wailed, flashing blue and white in her rear-view mirror.

Fifty years ago, lines of grim-faced men in high vis jackets prodded the moor with white sticks, smelt each one for traces of something unexplained, like farmers praying for lost sheep in snow, heads bent, devotional.

Myra's face had stared out from the tabloids on Formica kitchen tables. She was wild and square-jawed, her peroxide hair bleached to the colour of small white bones. Those children from Longsight, Gorton, Ashton were remembered by wives who held their daughters close as cutlery in baize-green drawers. And their men came home, stinking of methane from turning, turning the bog over like an eiderdown. Keith Bennet's still out there somewhere in the peat and sphagnum moss.

Midsummer

Today the temperature drops. Mist hangs over
the hills, horses feed in tall grass, elderflowers
bloom. The fever of summer, its constant
sneeze, its red-eye itch is soothed. Ferns
relax. Cats sleep all day on saggy cushions.
Here in the North, politicians argue over
global warming. Alice could show them rare
butterflies on the moors, swallows arriving a
month too soon, but not today. Not today.
She'll find her friends with their lovely
round bellies, share a bottle of chardonnay,
stuff their afternoon mouths with olives.

Hardcastle Crags

Enough to snuff the quick
Of her small heat out, but before the weight
Of stones and hills of stones could break
Her down to mere quartz grit in that stony light
She turned back.
— Sylvia Plath, 'Hardcastle Crags'

Alice is a giantess lying across Yorkshire, her legs bent in sleep, slightly parted, curving along the river. Mist settles in the creases of her skin, once full of the singing of shuttles. Twenty thousand flocked to her one Whit Tuesday. Smoke belched from chimneys where she snores; blackening the buildings, settling into lungs. Now picnickers, day-trippers, dog walkers and long-distance ramblers breathe in rain-washed air and lounge in the folds of her hay meadows.

She drives over a dead fox on the road one summer morning. She thinks of Hughes, Armitage and all those who have written in a blaze of red, thinking their fox was the only fox that mattered, its guts picked over by crows. Here are the murmurs of generations. Here are their bones.

The Gate-Opener

Alice tramps along the Pennine Way all summer and remote, Cumbrian sheep farms in the winter; lying in wait for ramblers, vagabonds, genuine Romanies, long-distance walkers, locals out for a stroll and fair-weather campers. She loves them all in separate ways. Now legendary throughout the North, she can negotiate any kind of five-bar, kissing or latch-key gate; unlocks padlocks with a hairpin that she keeps in her knickers; always shuts and secures each field after strangers.

She collects all the smiles, nods, pecks on the cheek and cheery thanks like bunches of wild flowers. One bright evening, Alice meets a man who has walked in solitude for miles and wants to tell another human being of the boggy moors, sodden clothes, the way the mist came down, his pedometer readings. The exact number of miles traversed.

Honeysuckle

Alice sings, *suckle me, my sugar man, my sticky-nectar lover. Suckle my honeybee nipples and let us remember that drowsy mooncalf state, propped up on feather pillows. My breasts are blue-veined, milk-white globes for once in my life. The evening is alive with hoverflies and the river darkens. Lick and nibble. Part my honeysuckle legs and suck all the sweetness from me with your delicate tongue.*

Nesting

And they scramble down the cobbled path to Lumb Falls and watch the river foam with Guinness-coloured water. And they saunter together through Heptonstall to the ruined church; witness Ted's crows nesting, Sylvia sleeping, her grave littered with plastic flowers and pens. And they lie together on her bed as Blackpool illuminates itself and girl-gangs in their tiaras knock back vodka.

Alice wears his mother's ring, feels the weight of carnelian and silver; senses a blessing as she kisses her new lover in her attic room.

Moss Eccles

Like Beatrix Potter and her love, they plant one red and one white waterlily for each other. This evening, whilst he sleeps, Alice casts off their rowing boat, comes to a halt at the centre of the tarn. She trails her fingertips through ripples and listens for lily petals unfolding. An oystercatcher whistles overhead, piercing the sky with short bursts of black and white delight. A mallard paddles across to the stand of larches. Alice watches the bird's silver V widen. A trout rises, chasing damselflies as they pulse electric blue across her bare feet. This stillness is curved like the tarn's floor. Beloved.

Bird's Foot Trefoil

When Alice's child is born, he's such a pea-shaped, yellow-jaundiced creature. Delicate as a young grouse picking his way through heather. She cradles him in wildflower meadows, wrapped in a felt blanket. He grows up strong and free, but he's a birdbrain, forgetting keys and coats and always putting his foot in his mouth.

Her three sisters have migrated to the bush, each with her tinfoil-wrapped lunch. She says to her son, *march up to the moors if you must, till you're footsore and full of grievance. It's a tough call, my pigeon-toed child. The topsoil's all blown off and is silting up the rivers. That bog, with its gullies and troughs, could swallow a boy.*

Crossroads

After Brexit, the crossing of barriers of all kinds becomes important. Straddling, hurdling, hanging votives on fences, cutting through wire or hammering concrete. Alice's mother had been at Greenham and wove ribbons into the barrier surrounding the air base. Her father had worked in Berlin when the Wall was punched through and the sky was brimming with freedom, firecrackers and laughter. She'd once tried to find a checkpoint in the wall in Belfast. It snaked poison through back gardens, past murals of armed men and curbstones painted red, white and blue.

Any wall begins in the mind, but the mind and heart can dissolve this hardening, just as salt crystals or honey dissolve into water, soothing our throats, making our voices sweeter.

Northern Powerhouse

The next day her son tries to explain quantum physics in the car. They're at the railway station and streams of commuters rush by, with their heads down and their collars turned up. He talks about particles acting as waves and Alice says, *where does the cat fit in all of this? Schrödinger and all that stuff about the cat, you know, shut in a sealed box along with something radioactive, a Geiger counter and a bottle of poison.* The boy shrugs his shoulders. *Google it if you want to know. I've had a long day.* He's now sixteen and this passes for in-depth conversation. So, they sit in silence and watch the northern commuters. Are they particles or waves? Manchester or Leeds? Alice wonders to herself but she doesn't speak out loud. Her son's too busy texting, with his head down and his collar turned up.

Clocks

Years later, Alice's husband wandered through rooms at night with a pair of pliers, wrenching the hands from their clocks. The whole place was suspended and Alice lost track of the hour, the moon rising like a blank-faced timepiece over the terraces and lines of washing stiff with frost. When they both thought it was morning, they rose in the dark to scrape ice from the car. The world was bent double as winter approached. *Don't like change*, he said. She nodded, couldn't risk the frozen bridge between them, in case she lost her footing, slipped into black water.

So, she humoured him. Hid her diamante-studded wristwatch under her pillow. She let them skate on the surface of their desperate conversations, tried to cook meals at appropriate intervals, hoped that they wouldn't become too nocturnal, wide eyed, padding about the flat. She stood at the window, stared at the toll route to Keighley skirting the moor, snaking down into the promise of the valley.

Mapping

When they met, their love was a beacon, silvering water with light. They were giddy and coastal, riding above the high, blue tideline.

Through the Trough of Bowland, he was her contour and field guide, her single-track road with passing places, her Leeds to Liverpool towpath. Each Bingley year together was a five-rise lock brimming over with love. And their Pennine Way was a dashing, red line of pleasure.

Now he's gone, Alice is all mud and shingle. She's Bridlington in winter. A dry canal without purpose or clay. A Flamborough Head lighthouse (disused.) Her days are flat rocks and sea cliffs. In his absence, she's out in The Wash: all marsh and saltings.

Wild Garlic and Detours

Alice can sense them all, pulling away from shadows of their loved ones, late in the evening when everything cools and lengthens and light catches the beech leaves.

The dead are walking backwards, skirting through the woods towards the Calder River and Crimsworth's deep ravine, murmuring to each other. Some are lingering near the water; some are climbing up through the banks of wild garlic, some gather bluebells to remind themselves of the living, to remind themselves that summer's nearly here and soon the meadowsweet will drown them all in scent.

Kippers

These fishbones. They fill her kitchen with the memory of the shoreline and taste of kelp and salt. Some are memories that stick in the throat, send Alice coughing and running to dial 999. Some bones are so sweet she spends a Saturday making a fishbone and feather necklace to wear to a party. She sails out across the street in a blue silk dress and calfskin slippers.

At dawn, she heads for the Northumberland coast. Remembers camping near the sea when love was tender and rockpool-clear. Turning through an arch, Alice drives headlong down the winding road to Craster harbour with its tiny semicircle of stone. Those *silver darlings* are dripping oil in the smoke-blackened sheds. They keep her memories kippered and sweet all winter.

True North

Out on the boat's bridge, Alice and her companion sit and watch the sunset, stare into that globe of light, half-swallowed by water as the sky blooms pink, then drains of colour. His white shirt glows. Alice knows his shoulders are sunburnt and tomorrow his skin will blister and peel. He radiates heat, smells of sweat, with his rolled-up sleeves and loosened tie to signal the end of the day. And without warning, without so much as a word between them, he leans towards her. She feels his forearm tighten across her breasts. Her back is pressed against him. Each pearlescent button imprints a circle on her spine. They sit still, clamped together in half-light, listening to the boat's diesel engine, herring gulls shrieking and circling.

They were lovers once and now hardly speak of this. But here at sea, he is her Polaris, her true North.

Biblical Lilies of the Field

I tell you I could speak again: whatever
returns from oblivion returns
to find a voice:
— Louise Glück, 'The Wild Iris'

Her mother's irises were once the jewels of
her riverbank garden with their bright tongues,
tissue-thin petals. They would bloom for a
few weeks in summer as soil warmed and
hawthorn blossom was spiked with songs of
coal tits and nesting blackbirds. After her
mother died, Alice transplanted them into a
plastic trough in the North and they had
never flowered since: tubers gnarled as arthritic
thumbs. Each spring, new blades offered up
the promise of that purple haze she'd
pictured, then slugs and snails feasted on
delicate shoots.

But Alice cannot throw them out. This year
she will buy fresh sand, gravel, lift and divide
with a sharp spade, lay them in a bed of
well-drained compost, in a sunnier spot.
She'll make beer traps, pick off snails, keep
her vigilance and drink green tea each morning
by the front porch as the days lengthen.

The Black Cat

Once the roof was stolen, Alice never wanted it to return. She watched the Milky Way, the Pleiades, the North Star. She woke, soaked to the skin, and was happy. Her thoughts lifted like dust, and she wrote page after page, now the stone tiles, roofing felt and gutters were missing. One evening, her face was snow-flaked. Darkness crept in and quilted her like an old friend. Orion turned and his scabbard jewelled the sky.

Alice grew to love the pale pink sunrise and the dawn chorus. She wrote of global warming, black cats, alleyways, murders and mistaken identities. She re-read *The Master and Margarita* well into the small hours:

Now, kindly ponder this question: What would your good do if evil didn't exist, and what would the earth look like if all the shadows disappeared? After all, shadows are cast by things and people. Here is the shadow of my sword. But shadows also come from trees and living beings…

Scarlet Pimpernel

Alice. Look at the state of her! Drowsy in a poppy field, overwhelmed by the humming, the midsummer humming of wild bees in a field of wheat. Three hares are hunkered down in the midday haze and, for the first time in years, she sees red carder bees, honeybees, field cuckoo bumblebees in this organic acre, set aside by a thoughtful Yorkshire farmer. Pesticides hang in clouds on the horizon of his neighbours' lands, but wildflowers, dormant in their parched soil, here run riot.

Alice's hares run for cover, scent a fox near the larch wood. The number of honeybee colonies has halved and she's disturbed. But loves the sexy nectar of June and its promise. The wonder of a more-than-human world! But the rest of us are out of kilter. Our future is on a trolley, under a white sheet. The G7 convene and cannot agree on a way forward. Trump will wheel climate change, Alice, Wonderland and all her ill-assorted kith and kin into the cold morgue and not give a shit. But right now, the world's humming. Cornflowers and scarlet pimpernel bloom.

Looking-Glass

All we have is happenstance and moments when contentment fills the air like a dozing cat with warm fur. The woman on the street is not Alice, but she walks with the same worry and frazzle. The girl Alice remembers seems so far removed from her current life. She returns in dreams in which Alice is freckled and full of pith and spite, freewheeling through lanes billowing with cow parsley, along canal paths and under railway bridges.

When did her youthful arrogance disappear? That self-belief and indignation at the human world's inability to heal itself? Maybe down a rabbit hole, or downstream with Ratty and Mole. Maybe through a looking-glass or into the folds of a red cloak.

Wonderland

'Oh I've had such a curious dream!' said Alice.
And she told her sister, as well as she could remember them,
all these strange Adventures of hers...
— Lewis Carroll, *Alice's Adventures in Wonderland*

Alice's North is all pound-shops and chip-
barms, *three curries and rice please* and fish-
supper Fridays; it's Yemen-in-Eccles and Halal-
in-Bolton; Hockney-in-Saltaire and Hepworth-
in-Wakefield.

It's fragile uplands and flooding and heather;
those diesel-fumed cities (no football or bitter);
it's permeable borders and plenty of rail-
track. Butts itself up against softness and
Scotland. It's Newcastle hen parties, Baltic
and blackthorn, a rare slipper orchid protected
in Malham.

Her wildness of language is gritstone and
millstone; volcanic in nature or limestone
dissolving in caverns and sinkholes; lost
snickets and ginnels, all morgrawm and mizzle:
don't mither me now, with your fracking and
twaddle.

Alice's North is a jut of the chin; dock-pudding in spring or a well-gutted kipper; mill-loft conversions and Brontë-themed day-trips; Branwell with gin in a Halifax tavern; Dorothy Wordsworth, fell-walking all weathers; unquenchable love for an obstinate brother. Her trailblazing, wonder-filled copperplate letters.

Acknowledgements

Some of these prose poems have previously been published in magazines, anthologies and web-journals including *Stride*, *The Valley Press Anthology of Yorkshire Poetry*, *Axon Journal* (Australia) *Rabbit Journal* (Australia), *The Bolton Review*, *Shadow Chest* (Beehive Poets, 2018), and in *Seam* (2015), *Pulse* (2016) and *Tract* (2017) from Recent Work Press, Australia. 'Crossroads' was runner up in the Tongues *&* Grooves Prose Poem Competition, 2018. Ten of these prose poems were short-listed in the Rialto Pamphlet Competition 2017 and two were published in *The Rialto* magazine in that same year.